Make Your Own
TEDDY BEARS

Instructions and Full-Size Patterns
for Jointed and Unjointed Bears
and Their Clothing

Doris King

Photographs by Ted Menten

Dover Publications, Inc., New York

Text copyright © 1985 by Doris King.
Photographs copyright © 1985 by Ted Menten.
All rights reserved under Pan American and International Copyright Conventions.

Published in Canada by General Publishing Company, Ltd., 30 Lesmill Road, Don Mills, Toronto, Ontario.
Published in the United Kingdom by Constable and Company, Ltd.

Make Your Own Teddy Bears: Instructions and Full-Size Patterns for Jointed and Unjointed Bears and Their Clothing is a new work, first published by Dover Publications, Inc., in 1985.

Manufactured in the United States of America
Dover Publications, Inc., 31 East 2nd Street, Mineola, N.Y. 11501

Library of Congress Cataloging-in-Publication Data

King, Doris.
  Make your own teddy bears.

(Dover needlework series)
  1. Soft toy making. 2. Teddy bears. I. Title.
TT174.3.K56 1985   745.592'4   85-15962
ISBN 0-486-24942-5 (pbk.)

MAKING THE BEARS

General Materials

TRADITIONAL FABRICS

The really old teddies were most frequently made from mohair. Mohair comes from Angora goats, which are natives of Turkey. Their hair grows to about 10 inches and, when woven into mohair, provides an easy-to-work fabric. The nap can be trimmed to lend character to teddy's face.

Another popular old fabric was alpaca. Processed from the hair of the South American llama or alpaca, the finished fabric has a short nap that feels very smooth and luxuriant. It is denser than mohair and not nearly as costly.

For truly traditional bear lovers, either of these fabrics may be found by checking with the local upholsterer. Keep in mind, though, that mohair can cost up to $100 per yard, and alpaca usually sells for around $35 to $40 per yard. Of course, you will only need about 3/8 of a yard to make your traditional teddy, and how many times will you ever do it again?

MODERN FABRICS

Before you decide to spend a fortune on genuine mohair or alpaca, perhaps you would be better advised to try a teddy in synthetic fur (also called fake fur, fur-by-the-yard or acrylic fur). Fur-by-the-yard comes in a nearly infinite variety of textures and colors.

Most fake fur fabrics have a knit backing. Some backings are more stable than others, so be sure to check the fabric to make sure it is not of the stretch variety. It can be downright embarrassing if you begin to stuff your teddy and the hide keeps stretching so that the bear winds up totally misshapen and looking like a very fat, hairy rhinoceros.

It's not even necessary to stick with hairy fabrics. Many very attractive teddies have been made from corduroy, calico, old coats, gingham, chintz, patchwork and so on. One seen recently was made with unbleached muslin and had no eyes, nose or mouth. This modern type is known as the generic teddy bear.

Whatever the fabric—let your imagination run rampant—just be sure it will take to being stuffed. Teddies tend to sulk if you can't make them come out close to their traditional shape.

STUFFING

The material selected to stuff the teddy will have a lot to do with the final appearance and feel. You must decide if you want a soft, cuddly, huggable teddy (these use soft stuffing materials such as cotton or polyester fiber), or a firmer, sturdier teddy with well-defined lines and character. The really old teddy bears were usually stuffed with excelsior and that is why many are still in shape some eighty years later.

Cotton batting is a good, inexpensive stuffing that is fairly easy to use. When using cotton, apply it evenly to avoid making lumps.

Polyester fiber is the most modern stuffing material available. Easier to use than cotton, it is kept on hand in most fabric stores and is relatively inexpensive.

Excelsior is a wood product made by shaving logs into long, curly strips. You've seen excelsior used as packing material for shipping fragile objects; taxidermists have used it for generations. One warning: excelsior is a very messy product to use; you'll find bits of wood shavings all over the house for days. The biggest value of this product is that it makes a firm shape when packed into your teddy. You will be better able to form the features and can expect them to hold their shape. Excelsior can usually be found either in a hard-

ware store or at a taxidermist's. In those parts of the country where homes are cooled with evaporative coolers, the cooler pads are made from excelsior. Purchase a couple of cooler pads, tear them apart and you're in business.

SEWING ON FUR FABRICS

Sewing on fur fabrics is not difficult; in fact, the fur can help disguise many minor sewing mistakes. Before you begin, however, there are a few special techniques you should know.

Fur fabrics have a very definite nap or "pile." Usually this pile runs lengthwise on the fabric; however, on some fur fabrics, it runs from selvage to selvage. To determine the direction of the pile, run your hand over the fabric. If it feels rough, you are going against the pile; if it is smooth, you are going with the pile. The pattern pieces should be placed on the fabric with the arrows pointing in the direction of the pile.

After the pattern pieces are arranged on the wrong side of the fabric, draw around each one with tailor's chalk or soft pencil. Use small sharp scissors to cut out the pieces, being careful to cut only the backing, not the pile. Cut each pattern piece singly; do not try to cut two pieces at once on a double layer of fabric.

The pieces can be stitched together by hand using a backstitch, or by machine using a straight stitch. For stronger seams, stitch each seam twice. After stitching the pieces together, you will probably find that some of the pile is caught in the stitching. With the blunt end of a needle, gently pull the pile out of the seam.

Pattern Pieces for Jointed and Unjointed Bears

Each pattern piece is lettered to correspond with the following list. All pieces are cut from fur fabric unless otherwise noted. The patterns begin on page 31.

Bear Body A	Side Head, jointed and un-jointed
Bear Body B	Center Head, jointed and un-jointed
Bear Body C	Ear, jointed and unjointed
Bear Body D	Back, jointed
Bear Body E	Front, jointed

Bear Body F	Back, unjointed
Bear Body G	Front, unjointed
Bear Body H	Inside Arm, jointed
Bear Body I	Paw Pad, jointed and unjointed (*cut from felt*)
Bear Body J	Inside Arm, unjointed
Bear Body K	Outside Arm, jointed and un-jointed
Bear Body L	Leg, unjointed
Bear Body M	Leg, jointed
Bear Body N	Foot Pad, jointed and unjointed (*cut from felt*)

Materials for Bear Bodies

For each jointed bear you will need:

    60″-wide fur fabric, ⅓ yard, for bear body
    Felt to match fur, ¼ yard, for paws
    Heavy-duty thread to match fur
    Dark brown embroidery floss or pearl cotton
      No. 5 for face details
    2 eyes
    Stuffing
    Ten 2″ joint washers (NOTE: These may be pur-
      chased from a doll-supply store, or cut from
      ⅛″ masonite with a 2″ hole saw.)
    Five ¾″ × ³⁄₃₂″ plated cotter pins (NOTE: Be sure
      to use plated cotter pins, as these will not
      rust.)

    Five 1½″ × ³⁄₃₂″ plated cotter pins
    Long-nose pliers
    Pattern pieces: A, B, C, D, E, H, I, K, M, N

For each unjointed bear you will need:

    60″-wide fur fabric, ⅜ yard, for bear
      body
    Felt to match fur, ¼ yard, for paws
    Heavy-duty thread to match fur
    Dark brown embroidery floss or pearl cotton
      No. 5 for face details
    2 eyes
    Stuffing
    Pattern pieces: A, B, C, F, G, I, J, K, L, N

Assembling the Jointed Bear

Side View

Front View

Approximately 18″ tall.

Pattern pieces include allowance for ¼″ seam all around. On each pattern piece, line up arrow with straight or crosswise grain of fabric so that arrow points in the direction of the pile. Cut all bear pattern pieces from fur or felt, as indicated. On each piece of cut fabric, mark location for arms, legs, ears, eyes with a piece of contrasting-color thread. Unless otherwise noted, stitch all pieces with right sides together. Clip or notch seam al-lowance of curves as needed so that they will turn smoothly.

HEAD

Step 1: Sew side pieces (pattern A) together from nose to neck (from * to *).

Step 2: Beginning at nose, spacing pins about ¼″ apart and easing to fit, pin center head piece (pattern B) in place (*Diagram 1*). Stitching each side separately, sew from nose to back of neck. Turn head to right side. If desired, the pile may be trimmed on the muzzle portion of the face.

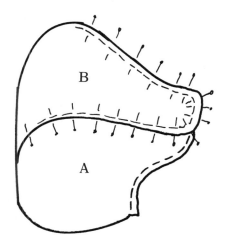

DIAGRAM 1

Step 3: Ears: Make 2. Using 2 pieces for each ear (pattern C), pin, then stitch, around sides and top. Turn ears to right side. Turn remaining raw edges to the inside and whip-stitch in place. (NOTE: Ears will not be attached to head until after head is stuffed.)

BODY

Step 4: Match, pin, then sew back (pattern D) and front (pattern E) side seams.

Step 5: Sew front/back units together (*Diagram 2*), leaving an opening for stuffing as indicated on pattern. Turn.

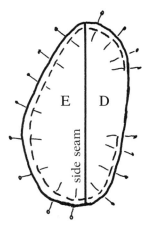

DIAGRAM 2

LEGS (Make 2)

Step 6: Using 2 pieces for each leg (pattern M), beginning at heel, first pin, then sew top and sides (*Diagram 3*). Leave bottom open.

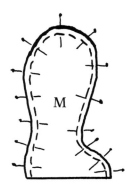

DIAGRAM 3

Step 7: Pin foot pad (pattern N) in place (*Diagram 4*). Sew with pad (felt) side up.

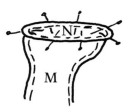

DIAGRAM 4

Step 8: When sewing is complete, place legs side by side with toes pointing outward. Cut turning and stuffing slits on inside of each leg as indicated on pattern. Turn. Work a few stitches at each end of slit to secure fabric.

ARMS (Make 2)

Step 9: Pin paw pad (pattern I) to inside arm (pattern H), matching as indicated; sew (*Diagram 5*).

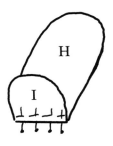

DIAGRAM 5

Step 10: Pin inside arm unit (pattern I/H) to outside arm (pattern K; *Diagram 6*). Sew. Cut turning and stuffing slit on inside of arm as indicated on pattern. Turn. Work a few stitches at each end of slit to secure fabric.

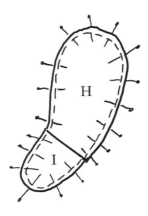

DIAGRAM 6

EYES

There are two types of eyes you can use for your teddy bear:
(1) A glass eye with a shank protruding through the fabric to be held in place with a detent washer. These may be purchased at many craft stores or from an outlet dealing in doll supplies; OR:
(2) Buttons which feature a metal loop on the back that is held in place with wire or thread.
Note: *Button eyes are not recommended if the toy is to be played with by small children.*

GLASS EYES

If you elect to use glass eyes, install them before stuffing the head. Make a small hole in the head at the eye marker, insert the shank and force the washer onto the shank from the inside of the head. You may want to use a piece of felt or other heavy material as a cushion between the washer and the back of the fabric (*Diagram 7*). When the eyes are in place, stuff the head firmly. Gather neck.

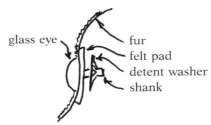

DIAGRAM 7

BUTTON EYES

If using button eyes, stuff the nose and about half the head firmly. Thread a large needle with a double strand of heavy-duty thread. From the inside of the head, push the needle through the stuffing and out the face at the eye mark; then, through the eyelet on the back of the button and back

through the stuffing. Tie securely, using a short piece of dowel for an anchor (*Diagram 8*). When the eyes are in place, finish stuffing head. Gather neck.

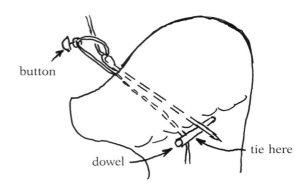

DIAGRAM 8

NOSE AND MOUTH

Beginning at A (*Diagram 9*), embroider satin stitches to fill the nose area. Bring the needle out at A, then insert it at B, bringing it out at C with the loop under the needle. Pull snugly to provide the nose border. Sew a stitch from C to D as

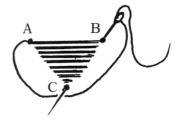

DIAGRAM 9

shown in *Diagram 10*. Next, bring the needle out at E, then insert it at F, bringing it out at D with the loop under the needle. Make a small stitch to secure last loop in place.

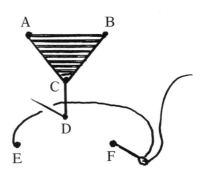

DIAGRAM 10

Varying the type of fabric used and the size of the eyes gives each of these bears a distinct personality.

JOINTS

Stuff arms and legs firmly; do not stuff body. Following the directions below, you will need a joint in each arm and leg, and in the neck.

Step 11: Insert a ¾″ cotter pin through the eye of a 1½″ pin; flare the ends with long-nose pliers to secure in place.

Step 12: Insert the 1½″ pin through a 2″ disc (*Diagram 11*).

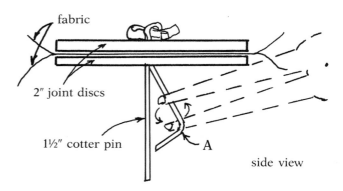

DIAGRAM 12

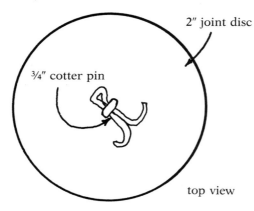

DIAGRAM 11

Step 13: Place disc and pin into the limb (as indicated on pattern) or into the head and, using strong thread, hand-stitch the opening closed.

Step 14: With an ice pick (or similar tool) make a hole in the body at each arm and leg marker. Push the 1½″ cotter pin through the hole or through the neck. At this point, take special care to watch for left and right sides.

Step 15: Slide another 2″ disc over the pin on the inside of the body.

Step 16: With long-nose pliers, twist the pin (*Diagram 12*). Apply enough pressure to create a great deal of tension, enough so that movement is difficult. (NOTE: The secret of making a proper

joint is tension. As you make the circular motion shown in Diagram 12, the pin should slide inward slightly through the hole in the disc. Once the body is stuffed, you will find you have enough room to move the limbs easily. If you have created enough tension in the joints, the arms, legs and head will stay where you put them. The completed joint inside the body should look like *Diagram 13*.)

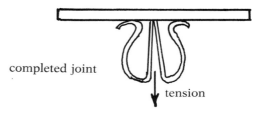

DIAGRAM 13

FINISHING

Check the arm, leg and neck joints for placement and secure attachments. Stuff the body firmly. When body is tightly packed, use heavy-duty thread to sew the back securely closed. Sew ears securely in place as indicated on pattern.

Assembling the Unjointed Bear

Front View

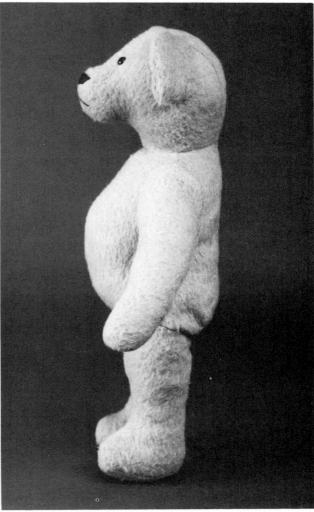

Side View

Approximately 18″ tall.

Pattern pieces include allowance for ¼″ seam all around. On each pattern piece, line up arrow with straight or crosswise grain of fabric so that arrow points in the direction of the pile. Cut all bear pattern pieces from fur or felt, as indicated. On each piece of cut fabric, mark location for ears and eyes with a piece of contrasting-color thread. Unless otherwise noted, stitch all pieces with right sides together. Clip or notch seam allowance of curves as needed so that they will turn smoothly.

HEAD

Steps 1 through 3: Work same as for jointed bear, leaving 2″ of head seam open in back.

BODY

Step 4: Pin and sew darts on backs (pattern F).

Step 5: Pin, then sew lower portion of back pieces together. (NOTE: The stuffing opening and seam above it will be closed later.)

Step 6: Pin and sew front pieces (pattern G) together at center.

Step 7: Match, pin and sew shoulder seams. Sew side seams. Do not turn.

JOINING HEAD TO BODY

Step 8: Match front and rear seams of head and body. Easing to fit as necessary, sew neck seam. Do not turn.

ARMS (Make 2)

Step 9: Pin, then sew dart on inside arm (pattern J).

Step 10: Sew straight edge of paw pad (pattern I) to inside arm (pattern J), matching as indicated.

Step 11: Pin and sew J/I to outside arm (pattern K), easing to fit. Leave upper end open to attach arm to body. Turn.

LEGS (Make 2)

Step 12: Using 2 pieces for each leg (pattern L), pin and then sew front and back seams.

Step 13: Pin and sew on foot pad (pattern N) as in Step 7 of jointed bear. Turn.

JOINING ARMS AND LEGS TO BODY

Step 14: Insert legs into body and align with side and center seams. (NOTE: Toes must be pointing forward inside the chest.) Easing to fit, pin and sew legs to body. Using heavy-duty thread, hand-stitch crotch for reinforcement.

Step 15: Insert arms into body with paws toward the front. Align center of outer arm with shoulder seam; align center of inner arm (dart) with side seam. Easing to fit, sew arms in place.

Step 16: Sew back seam from top of head opening to top of stuffing opening. Turn bear right side out.

Step 17: Work eyes and embroidered face details in place as described on page 8.

Step 18: Stuff bear firmly. With heavy-duty thread, sew back opening closed.

Step 19: Sew ears in place as indicated on pattern.

Pajamas

Suit, Shirt and Bow Tie

Reversible Bonnet and Stole

Jogging Suit

Dress

Pinafore

Jogging Shorts and Tank Top

Apron and Chef's Cap

Slacks and Blouse

Long Shorts and Shirt

CLOTHES

Pattern Pieces for Clothes

Each pattern piece is lettered to correspond with the following list. The patterns begin on page 47.

Clothes A   Jacket Front and Jacket Facing
Clothes B   Jacket Back, Shirt Back, Vest Back
Clothes C   Collar
Clothes D   Sleeve for Jacket, Pajama Top, Jogging Pullover, Shirt and Blouse
Clothes E   Shirt Front
Clothes F   Bow-Tie Bow
Clothes G   Bow-Tie Knot
Clothes H   Vest Front and Vest Facing
Clothes I   Vest Pocket
Clothes J   Bonnet
Clothes K   Front for Jogging Shorts, Long Shorts, Slacks and Suit Pants
Clothes L   Back for Jogging Shorts, Long Shorts, Slacks and Suit Pants
Clothes M   Jogging Pullover and Pajama Top, Front and Back
Clothes N   Jogging Pants and Pajama Bottom
Clothes O   Dress Front and Back
Clothes P   Dress Sleeve
Clothes Q   Apron
Clothes R   Apron Pocket
Clothes S   Pinafore
Clothes T   Pinafore Pocket
Clothes U   Tank-Top

There are no patterns for the stole or the chef's cap. Directions for the stole are included with the directions for the bonnet. Directions for the chef's cap are included with the directions for the apron.

Assembling Clothes

All clothes pattern pieces include allowance for ¼″ seam all around. For each pattern piece, line up arrows with straight grain of fabric. Unless otherwise noted, stitch all pieces with right sides together. Clip or notch seam allowance of curves as needed, so that they will turn smoothly. Finish any raw edges that are not folded into hems with straight stitch, zigzag stitch or hand overcast stitch. Press all seams open as you work.

SUIT

For jacket, vest and pants you will need:
  Lightweight wool, ⅓ yard
  Thread to match fabric
  ⅜″-wide elastic, 5¼″
  5 buttons, ⅜″ in diameter
  3 snaps
  Pattern pieces: For jacket: A, B, D
            For vest: B, H, I
            For pants: K, L

Step 1: Cut all pattern pieces, including facings for vest and jacket, from fabric as indicated on patterns.

JACKET

Step 2: Sew jacket-front pieces (pattern A) together at back of collar (from * to *). In the same manner, sew jacket-facing pieces together (same pattern).

Step 3: Sew jacket front and collar (pattern A) to jacket back (pattern B) at shoulders and back of neck, clipping seam allowance of collar as necessary.

Step 4: Pin facing to front edge of jacket and around collar. Sew in place. Turn facing to inside.

Step 5: Tack edge of facing to jacket.

Step 6: Pin sleeves (pattern D) to armholes, easing as necessary to fit. Sew in place.

Step 7: Sew side and underarm seams.

Step 8: Fold a ½″ hem on sleeves and around jacket bottom. Turn raw edge to the inside. Sew hems.

Step 9: Mark jacket front for 2 buttons, evenly spaced. Work buttonholes opposite marks. Sew buttons in place.

VEST

Step 10: Finish inner edges of facings.

Step 11: Sew facings to front and lower edges of vest front pieces (Pattern H). Turn facings to inside.

Step 12: Sew vest fronts (pattern H) to vest back (pattern B) at shoulders. Fold and stitch a ¼″ hem on back neck.

Step 13: Fold and stitch a ¼″ hem at armholes.

Step 14: Sew side seams.

Step 15: Fold and stitch a ¼″ hem on lower edge.

Step 16: Fold vest pocket (pattern I) in half as indicated. Sew sides, then turn. Fold remaining raw edge to the inside and slip-stitch in place. Sew to vest.

Step 17: Mark vest front for 3 buttons, evenly spaced. Sew on buttons, then sew snaps at back of each button for front closing.

PANTS

Step 18: On the pants front pieces (pattern K), sew center seam (from * to *). Topstitch simulated fly along line indicated on pattern. In the same manner, on pants back (pattern L), sew center seam (from * to *).

Step 19: Working on pants back, fold a ¼″ hem along the top edge and stitch in place. Stretching elastic as necessary to fit, sew elastic along waist edge.

Step 20: As indicated on pants front (pattern K), sew pleat at each side.

Step 21: Cut a 1″ × 9″ piece of fabric for front facing. With right sides of pants front and facing together, sew. Turn facing to inside and topstitch.

Step 22: Matching edges of front and back, sew side seams.

Step 23: Fold a ¼″ hem at bottom of each leg and sew in place.

Step 24: Sew inner leg seams.

SHIRT OR BLOUSE

For each shirt or blouse you will need:
  Cotton fabric, ¼ yard
  Thread to match fabric
  3 buttons, ⅜″ in diameter
  3 snaps
  Rickrack (optional)
  Pattern pieces: B, C, D, E

Step 1: Cut all pattern pieces from fabric.

Step 2: Sew collar pieces (pattern C) together along sides and outer (unnotched) edge. Clip corners as necessary. Turn. If desired, sew rickrack around collar, close to edge.

Step 3: Sew back (pattern B) to fronts (pattern E) at shoulders.

Step 4: Matching notches, baste collar to neck edge, easing collar to fit.

Step 5: Right sides together, fold facings on line indicated on pattern E and align to notches. Stitch across entire neck edge; stitch across bottom of facings, ⅜″ from edge. Turn facings to inside.

Step 6: Press neck seam towards shirt and top-stitch to hold in place.

Step 7: Sew sleeves (pattern D) to armholes. Fold ⅝″ sleeve hem; turn raw edge to inside and sew. If desired, sew rickrack across each sleeve.

Step 8: Sew underarm and side seams.

Step 9: Fold ⅜″ hem at bottom; turn raw edge to inside. Sew in place.

Step 10: Sew 3 buttons, evenly spaced, to front. Sew snaps at back of each button.

BOW TIE

For bow tie you will need:
    Satin fabric, 3″ × 8″
    Thread to match fabric
    ¼″-wide elastic, 10″
    Snap
    Pattern pieces: F, G

Step 1: Cut all pattern pieces from fabric.

Step 2: Fold ⅛″ on each short end of bow (pattern F) to wrong side.

Step 3: Right sides together, fold ends of bow to center along broken lines indicated on pattern. Stitch across top and bottom. Turn bow right side out; slip-stitch opening.

Step 4: Fold raw edges of knot (pattern G) to wrong side. Pin knot around bow, pleating bow slightly at center. Center elastic at back of bow. Hand-stitch all pieces together (*Diagram 14*).

Step 5: Sew snap at ends of elastic.

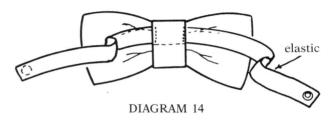

DIAGRAM 14

REVERSIBLE BONNET AND STOLE

For the bonnet and stole you will need:

54″-wide lightweight white wool, ½ yard

Pink fabric, ¼ yard for bonnet

1½″-wide beige gathered lace, 2 yards for stole

¾″-wide pink gathered lace, 2½ yards for bonnet

¾″-wide beige flat lace beading, 2¼ yards for stole and bonnet

⅜″-wide pink ribbon, 3 yards for stole and bonnet

1″-wide pink satin ribbon, 1 yard for bonnet ties

¼″-wide pink satin braid, ½ yard for bonnet

Several fabric flowers for bonnet

Thread to match fabrics and laces

Lightweight cardboard

18″ by 36″ sheet of paper to make stole pattern

Pattern piece: J for bonnet; directions for making stole pattern are below.

STOLE

Step 1: To make pattern: Draw a 15″ × 30″ rectangle on paper. Mark center of one long edge; draw a line from center mark to each end of other long edge to make triangle. Draw a curve on center point of triangle (*Diagram 15*).

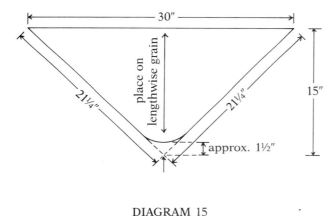

DIAGRAM 15

Step 2: Using the pattern just constructed, cut 2 stoles from white fabric.

Step 3: Leaving an opening for turning, allowing ¼″ seam all around, sew the 2 stole pieces together. Turn. Slip-stitch opening closed.

Step 4: Turning under and lapping raw ends, pin, then stitch, 1½″-wide beige gathered lace evenly around stole.

Step 5: Weave ⅜″-wide ribbon through holes in lace beading. Pin beading around stole over edge of gathered lace. Turning under and lapping ends, stitch beading in place.

Step 6: Using about 12″ of ⅜″-wide ribbon for each, make two bows. Tack one at each point of long edge.

BONNET

Step 7: From bonnet pattern (pattern J), cut 1 piece cardboard (same size) and 2 pieces white fabric (¼″ larger all around for seam allowance).

Step 8: Sew pieces of white fabric together around long curved front edge (leave shorter back edge open). Turn.

Step 9: Insert cardboard. Turn raw edge of fabric to inside and slip-stitch in place.

Step 10: Cut a piece of ¾″-wide pink gathered lace and slip-stitch across back of bonnet.

Step 11: Cut two 50″ lengths of ¾″-wide pink gathered lace. Pleat one 50″ piece evenly. Turning under raw ends, slip-stitch pleated lace around long curved front edge, covering raw ends of lace on back. In the same manner, sew remaining 50″ length to underside of bonnet on long curved edge. Turning in ends, sew ¼″-wide pink satin trim over edge of lace on top of bonnet.

Step 12: Pin lace beading over edge of lace on back of bonnet. Turn under raw ends and sew in place.

Step 13: Cut 2 pieces of 1″-wide pink satin ribbon. Sew one piece at each edge for ties.

Step 14: Cut a 4½″ × 45″ piece of pink fabric. Following *Diagram 16*, taper ends. Baste a ½″ hem all around.

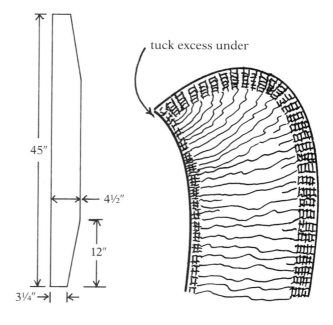

DIAGRAM 16   DIAGRAM 17

Step 15: Using matching-color thread, spacing rows about ¼" apart, sew 5 rows of gathering across long tapered edge, 2 rows across remaining edge. Pull gathering threads tightly enough so that piece fits as a lining on inside of bonnet. Slipstitch gathered piece to inside of bonnet, turning excess fabric to the wrong side (*Diagram 17*).

Step 16: Sew flowers in place on top of bonnet.

SLACKS

For slacks you will need:
    Cotton fabric, ¼ yard
    Thread to match fabric
    ⅜"-wide elastic, 5¼"
    Pattern pieces: K, L

Step 1: Cut all pattern pieces from fabric.

Step 2: On the slacks front pieces (pattern K), sew center seam (from * to *). In the same manner, on slacks back pieces (pattern L), sew center seam (from * to *).

Step 3: Working on slacks back, fold a ¼" hem along the top edge and stitch in place. Stretching elastic as necessary to fit, sew elastic along waist edge.

Step 4: As indicated on slacks front (pattern K), sew pleat at each side.

Step 5: Cut a 1" × 9" piece of fabric for front facing. With right sides of slacks front and facing together, sew. Turn facing to inside and topstitch.

Step 6: Matching edges of front and back, sew side seams.

Step 7: Fold a ¼" hem at bottom of each leg and sew in place.

Step 8: Sew inner leg seam.

SHORTS

For each pair of jogging shorts or long shorts you will need:
    Cotton fabric, ¼ yard
    Thread to match fabric for long shorts; contrasting-color thread for jogging shorts
    ⅜"-wide elastic, ⅓ yard
    Pattern pieces: K, L

Step 1: Cut all pattern pieces from fabric.

Step 2: Sew center seam on back pieces (pattern L), then center seam on front pieces (pattern K).

Step 3: Sew side, then inner leg seams.

Step 4: Fold waist edge ¼" to the inside. Cut a 12" length of elastic and, stretching elastic as necessary to fit, sew in place around waist.

Step 5: For jogging shorts only: Turn a ⅜" hem on each leg; fold raw edge to the inside; sew hem. For long shorts only: Turn a 1" hem on each leg; fold raw edge to the inside; sew. Turn up cuff and tack in place at sides.

PAJAMAS AND JOGGING SUIT

For each pajama set or jogging suit (pullover and pants) you will need:
  Flannel or knit fabric, ¼ yard
  11"-wide or 18"-wide knit cuff fabric, ¼ yard for pajamas; ½ yard for jogging suit
  Thread to match fabric
  2 snaps
  ¼"-wide elastic, 10"
  Appliqué for jogging suit (optional)
  Pattern pieces: D, M, N

Step 1: Cut all pattern pieces from fabric.

Step 2: For pajamas, cut knit cuff fabric crosswise into 2"-wide strips; for jogging suit, cut cuff fabric crosswise into 3½"-wide strips.

PAJAMA AND PULLOVER TOP

Step 3: Sew shoulder seams to join front and back pieces (pattern M).

Step 4: Sew sleeves (pattern D) to armholes.

Step 5: Cut an 8" piece of knit cuff fabric for neck and a 4½" piece for each sleeve. Fold each piece of cuff in half with long edges together. Stretching cuff to fit, sew to appropriate raw edge.

Step 6: Sew underarm and side seams. For jogging suit only: Cut a 16" piece of cuff fabric; fold in half and sew to lower edge. Sew back seam as indicated on pattern.

Step 7: Fold raw edges on back opening and slipstitch in place. For pajamas only: Fold ⅝" hem on lower edge, turn raw edge in and sew in place.

Step 8: Sew 2 snaps at back opening.

Step 9 (optional): Sew appliqué to front of jogging suit.

PAJAMA BOTTOM AND JOGGING PANTS

Step 10: Sew center front seam, then center back seam for pants (pattern N).

Step 11: Cut a 5" piece of knit cuff fabric for each leg. Fold cuff in half with long edges together. Stretching cuff to fit, sew to lower edge of each leg.

Step 12: Fold raw edge at waist to inside. Pin elastic to waist, stretching as necessary to fit, and sew.

Step 13. Sew inner leg seam.

DRESS

For the dress you will need:
  Calico fabric or organdy, ½ yard
  Bias tape to match fabric
  Thread to match fabric
  Baby rickrack, 3 yards; OR contrasting color thread for decorative stitching
  2 snaps
  Pattern pieces: O, P

Step 1: Cut all pattern pieces from fabric.

Step 2: Matching markings AA and BB of dress (pattern O) and sleeves (pattern P), sew sleeves to dress.

Step 3: Sew 3 rows of gathering stitches around neck as indicated on patterns. Try dress on bear and adjust gathering to fit neck. Fold and pin a ¼" hem at back neck opening. Folding ends of rickrack to inside of dress, sew rickrack over each gathering line; OR stitch over each line using a decorative machine stitch and contrasting-color thread.

Step 4: Cut a piece of bias tape ¾" longer than neck. Turning in ends of tape, fold tape over raw edge at neck and sew.

Step 5: Fold a ½" hem on each sleeve; turn raw edge to inside. Stitch rickrack across sleeve just below top of hem; OR stitch hem in place using a decorative machine stitch and contrasting-color thread.

Step 6: Sew underarm and side seams.

Step 7: Fold bottom hem as indicated on dress (pattern O); turn raw edge to inside. Stitch rickrack across dress just below top of hem; OR stitch hem in place using a decorative machine stitch and contrasting-color thread.

Step 8: Sew back seam as indicated on dress (pattern O).

Step 9: Sew snaps to back opening.

APRON AND CHEF'S CAP

For the apron and chef's cap you will need:
  Cotton fabric, ⅓ yard
  Bias tape to match fabric, 1½ yards
  Thread to match fabric

Medium-weight iron-on facing, 2¼″ × 11″
Pattern pieces: Q and R for apron; directions for cutting cap pieces are below.

APRON

Step 1: Cut pattern pieces for apron (pattern Q) and pocket (pattern R) from fabric.

Step 2: Fold side edge of apron ⅛″ to the wrong side, then fold ⅛″ again to form a double-fold hem. Sew sides.

Step 3: Fold bottom edge ¾″ to wrong side. Turn raw edge under and sew hem.

Step 4: Cut a piece of bias tape to fit along top of apron. Fold tape over raw edge and sew.

Step 5: Cut 2 pieces of bias tape, each about 24″ long. Center a length of folded tape over each curved edge (armhole) and sew. (NOTE: The extra lengths at top tie around bear's neck; the side lengths tie at back.)

Step 6: Fold pocket (pattern R) at top as indicated, turn raw edge to the inside and stitch. Press remaining raw edges of pocket ⅛″ to the back; sew pocket on apron front.

CHEF'S CAP

Step 7: From fabric, cut a circle 11″ in diameter and a 4½″ × 11″ strip.

Step 8: Arrange iron-on facing on lower half of 11″-long fabric strip and iron.

Step 9: Sew ends of strip together to form a circle. Press under ¼″ on long raw edges; fold circle in half to form a double band. Set piece aside.

Step 10: Working around edge of large circle, sew 2 gathering rows, the first about ⅛″ from edge, the second about ¼″ from edge. Draw up gathering threads until piece fits easily into band.

Step 11: Place band over edge of gathered circle—just enough to cover gathering stitches. Topstitch band to cap.

PINAFORE

For the pinafore you will need:
    Cotton fabric, ⅓ yard
    ⅜″-wide gathered lace, 2½ yards
    ½-wide satin ribbon, 1 yard
    4 buttons, ¼″ in diameter
    Pattern pieces: S, T

Step 1: Cut pattern pieces from fabric.

Step 2: Cut a piece of lace long enough to fit around entire outer edge of pinafore.

Step 3: Working on right side of pinafore (pattern S), matching raw edge of fabric and gathered edge of lace and lapping ends of lace, baste lace in place.

Step 4: Pin the 2 pinafore pieces with right sides together. Cut two 12″ pieces of ribbon and, with ribbon to the inside, pin as indicated on pattern.

Step 5: Leaving an opening at bottom for turning, sew around entire edge of pinafore. Turn. Slip-stitch opening closed.

Step 6: Each of the two pockets (pattern T) uses 2 pieces. Sandwich lace around side and bottom edges the same as on pinafore, and sew pieces together, leaving top edge open. Turn pocket, turn in raw edges and slip-stitch together. Topstitch pockets in place as indicated on pattern.

Step 7: Tack front and back shoulder straps together. Sew a button at each shoulder. Sew a button to each pocket as indicated on pattern.

Step 8: With remaining ribbon, tie a bow and sew in place at neck.

TANK TOP

For each tank top you will need:
    Open-weave fabric, ¼ yard
    Cotton fabric for lining, ¼ yard (optional)
    Thread to match fabric
    Contrasting-color bias tape
    Appliqué (optional)
    Snap
    Pattern piece: U

Step 1: Cut 1 front and 1 back (pattern U) from open-weave fabric. To line the top, cut a front and back from lining fabric and baste to wrong side of open-weave pieces.

Step 2: Cut a piece of bias tape to fit back opening. Fold tape over raw edge at back; sew.

Step 3: Sew front and back together at shoulders. Cut a piece of bias tape to fit around neck. Fold tape over raw edge at neck; turn in ends and sew in place. In the same manner, cut and sew bias tape to armholes.

Step 4: Sew side seams.

Step 5: Fold a ⅜″ hem around lower edge. Turn raw edge to inside; sew hem.

Step 6: Sew snap to top of back opening. If desired, sew on appliqué.

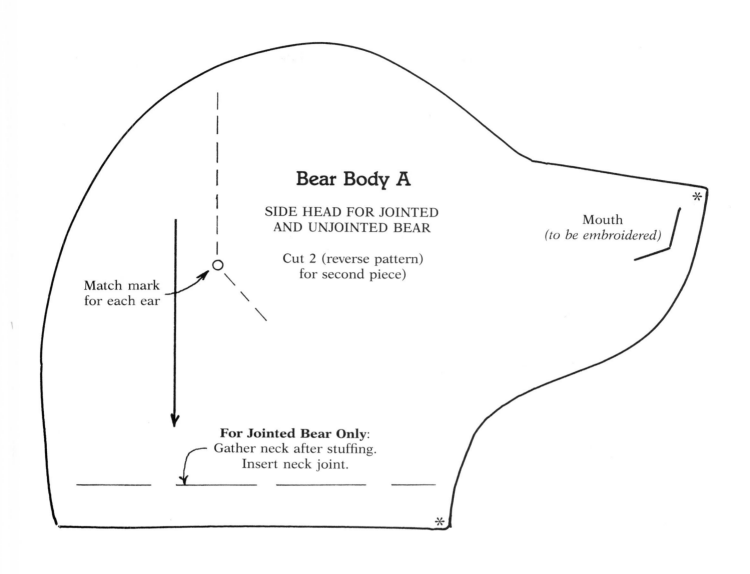

Bear Body A

SIDE HEAD FOR JOINTED AND UNJOINTED BEAR

Cut 2 (reverse pattern)
for second piece)

Mouth
(to be embroidered)

Match mark
for each ear

For Jointed Bear Only:
Gather neck after stuffing.
Insert neck joint.

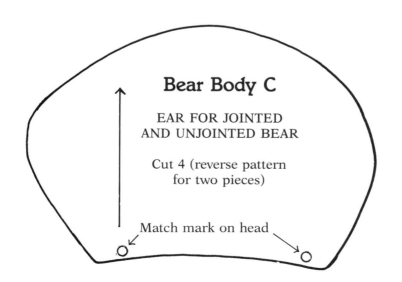

Bear Body C

EAR FOR JOINTED AND UNJOINTED BEAR

Cut 4 (reverse pattern
for two pieces)

Match mark on head

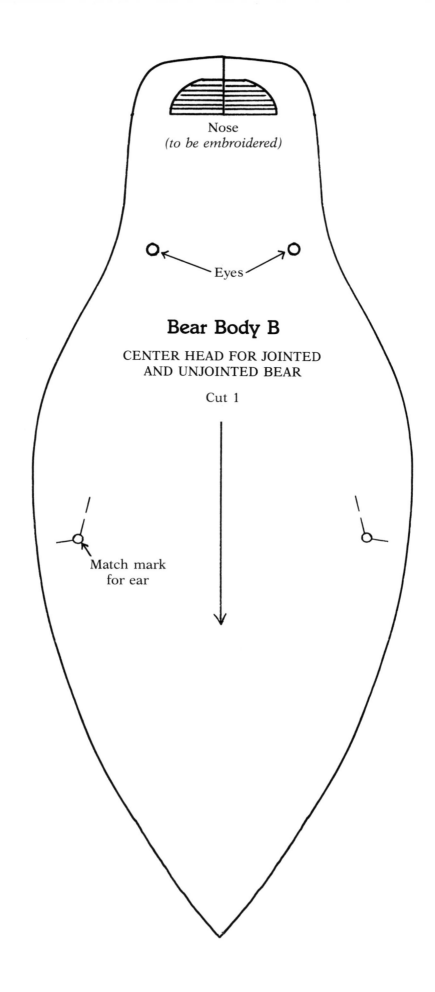

Nose
(to be embroidered)

Eyes

Bear Body B

CENTER HEAD FOR JOINTED
AND UNJOINTED BEAR

Cut 1

Match mark
for ear

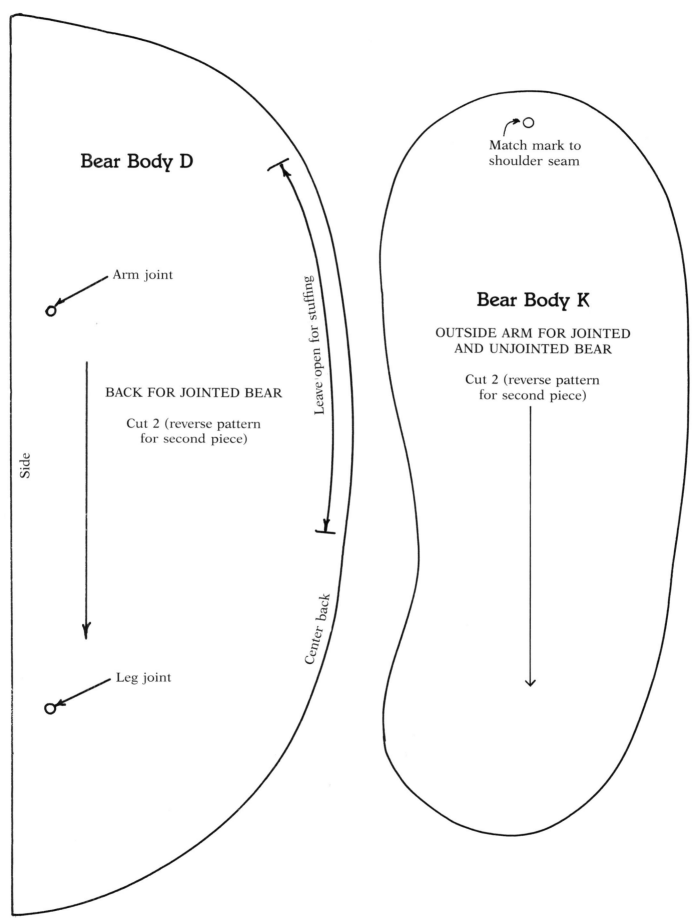

Bear Body D

Arm joint

BACK FOR JOINTED BEAR

Cut 2 (reverse pattern
for second piece)

Leave open for stuffing

Center back

Side

Leg joint

Match mark to
shoulder seam

Bear Body K

OUTSIDE ARM FOR JOINTED
AND UNJOINTED BEAR

Cut 2 (reverse pattern
for second piece)

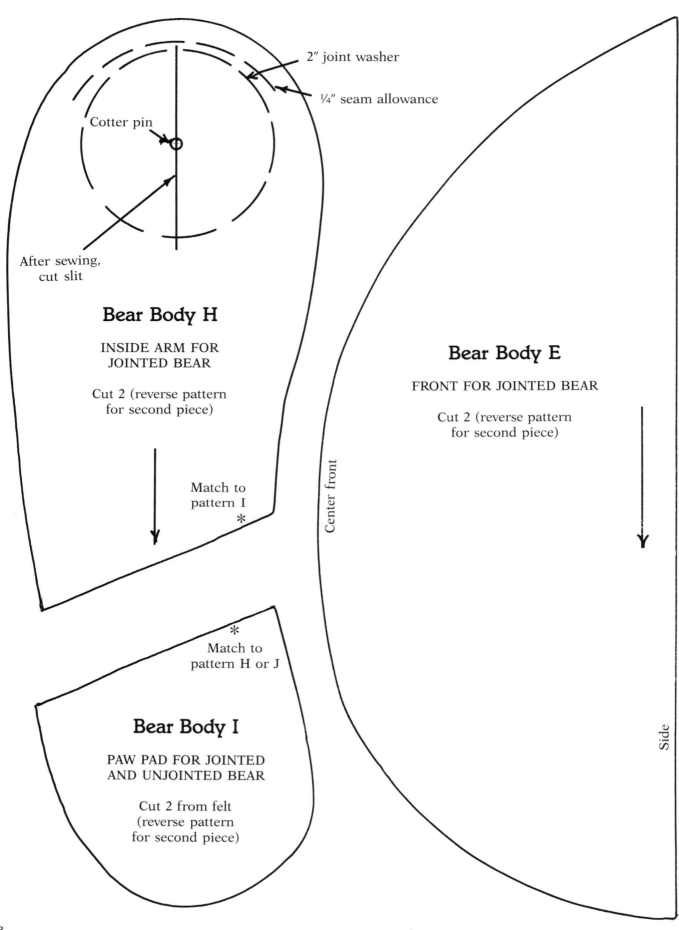

2″ joint washer

¼″ seam allowance

Cotter pin

After sewing,
cut slit

Bear Body H

INSIDE ARM FOR
JOINTED BEAR

Cut 2 (reverse pattern
for second piece)

Match to
pattern I

*

Center front

Bear Body E

FRONT FOR JOINTED BEAR

Cut 2 (reverse pattern
for second piece)

*
Match to
pattern H or J

Bear Body I

PAW PAD FOR JOINTED
AND UNJOINTED BEAR

Cut 2 from felt
(reverse pattern
for second piece)

Side

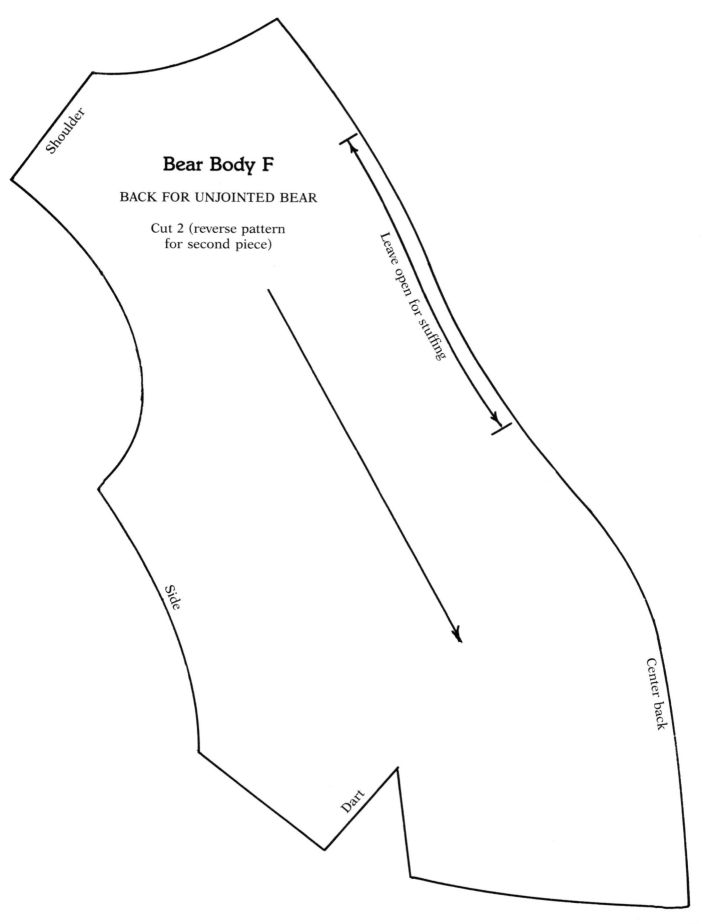

Bear Body F

BACK FOR UNJOINTED BEAR

Cut 2 (reverse pattern
for second piece)

Shoulder

Leave open for stuffing

Side

Center back

Dart

39

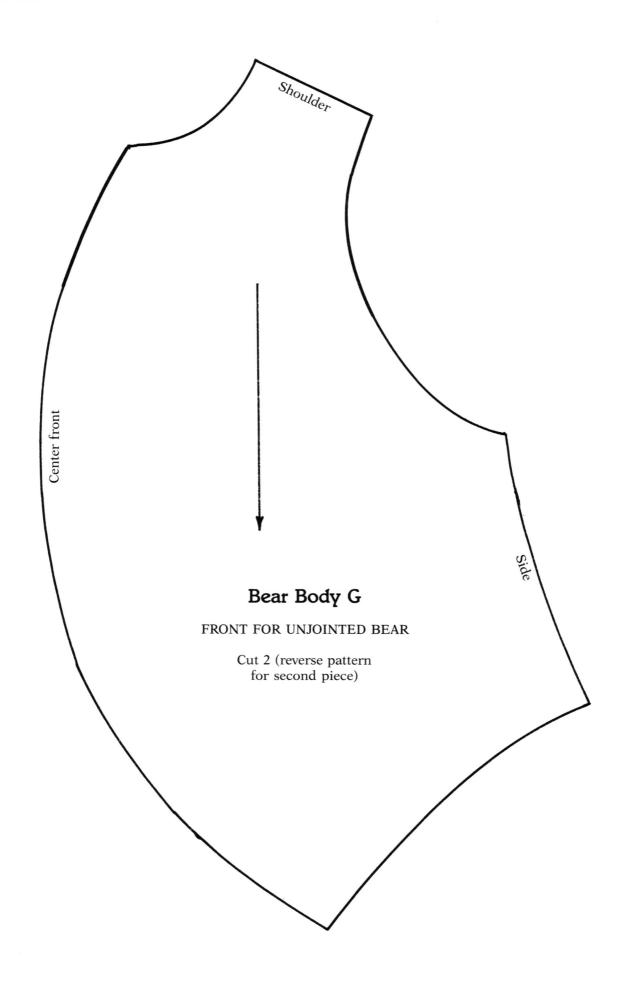

Shoulder

Center front

Side

Bear Body G

FRONT FOR UNJOINTED BEAR

Cut 2 (reverse pattern
for second piece)

42

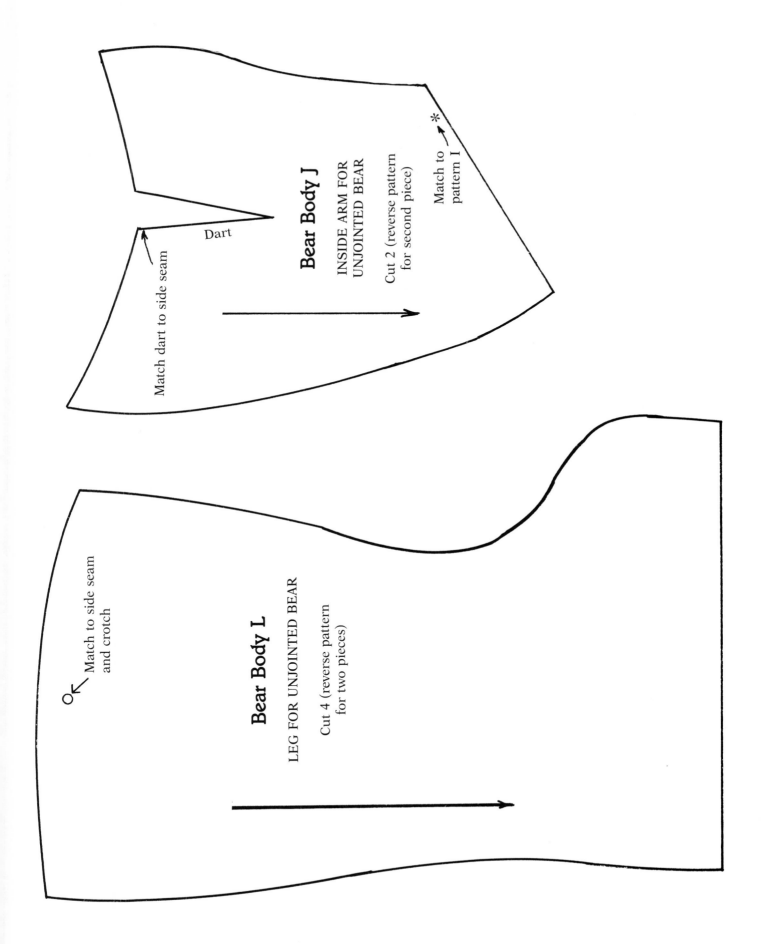

Dart

Match dart to side seam

Bear Body J

INSIDE ARM FOR
UNJOINTED BEAR

Cut 2 (reverse pattern
for second piece)

Match to
pattern I

*

Match to side seam
and crotch

Bear Body L

LEG FOR UNJOINTED BEAR

Cut 4 (reverse pattern
for two pieces)

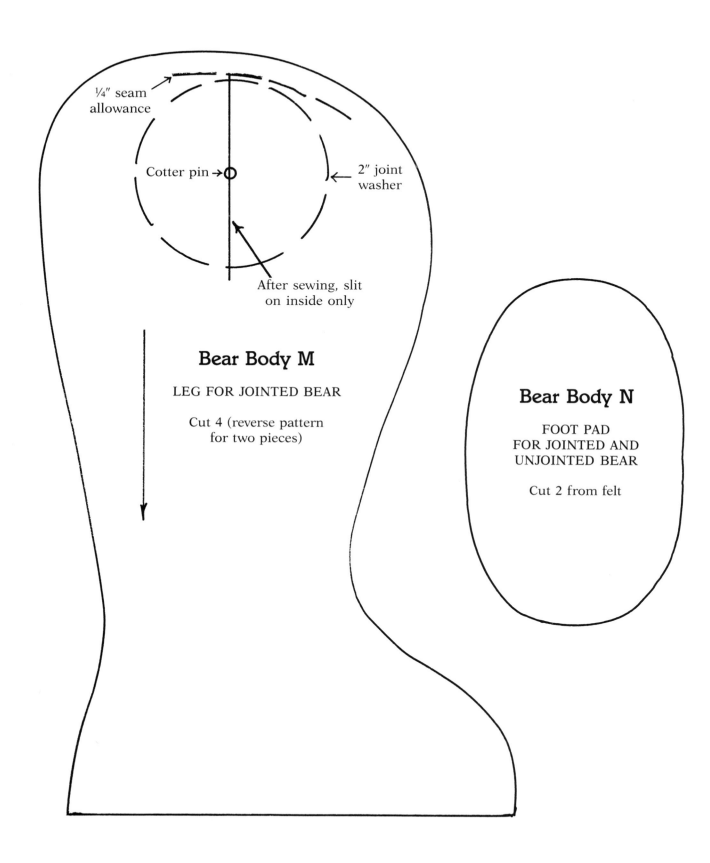

¼" seam allowance

Cotter pin →

2" joint washer

After sewing, slit on inside only

Bear Body M

LEG FOR JOINTED BEAR

Cut 4 (reverse pattern for two pieces)

Bear Body N

FOOT PAD
FOR JOINTED AND
UNJOINTED BEAR

Cut 2 from felt

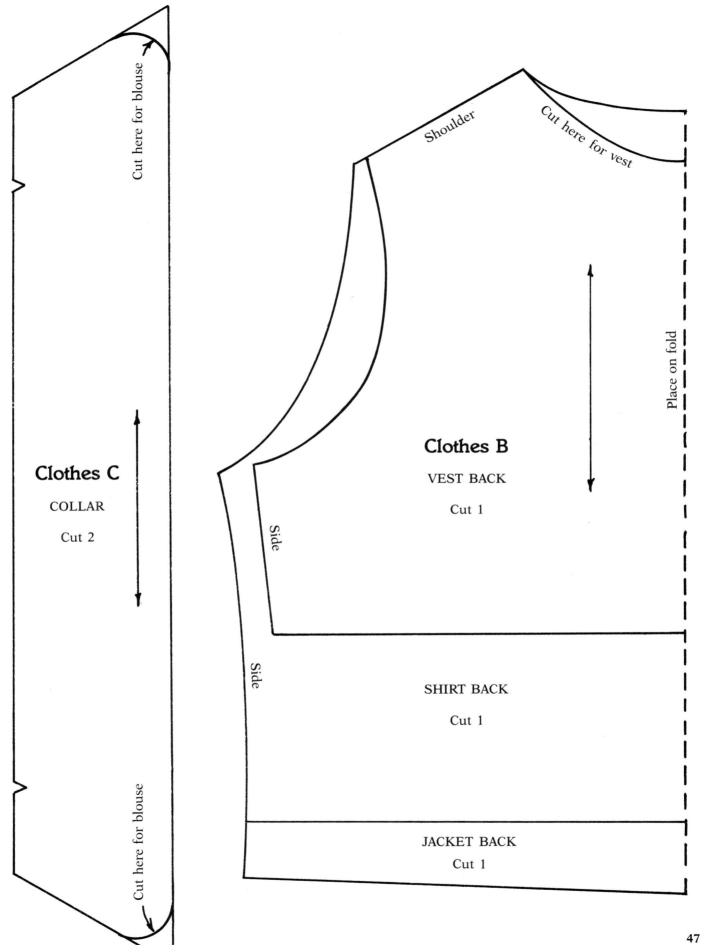

Cut here for blouse

Clothes C

COLLAR

Cut 2

Cut here for blouse

Shoulder

Cut here for vest

Place on fold

Clothes B

VEST BACK

Cut 1

Side

Side

SHIRT BACK

Cut 1

JACKET BACK

Cut 1

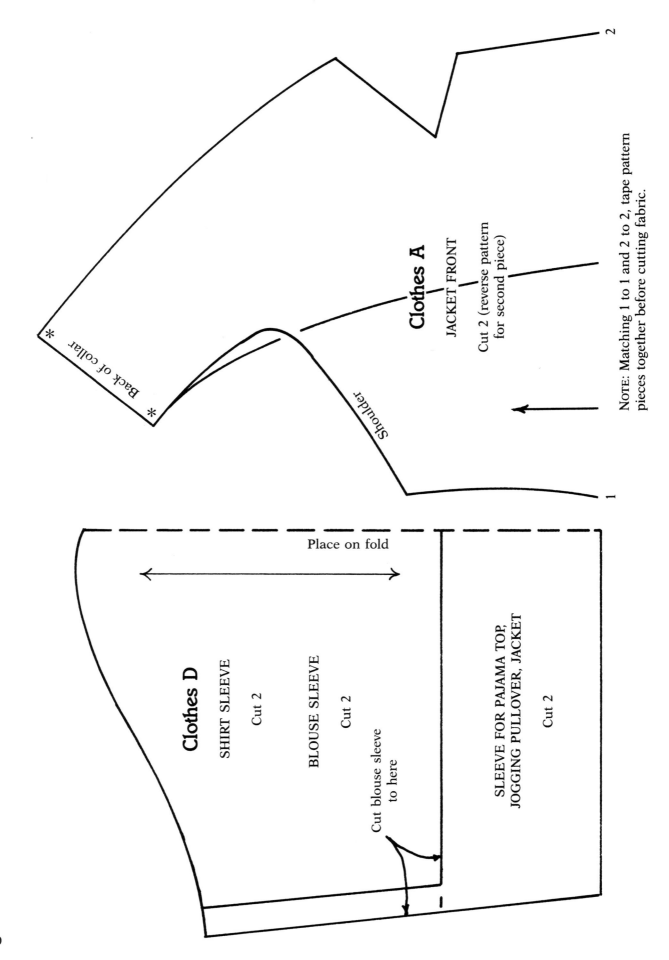

Clothes A

JACKET FRONT

Cut 2 (reverse pattern for second piece)

Back of collar

Shoulder

NOTE: Matching 1 to 1 and 2 to 2, tape pattern pieces together before cutting fabric.

2

1

Clothes D

SHIRT SLEEVE

Cut 2

BLOUSE SLEEVE

Cut 2

SLEEVE FOR PAJAMA TOP, JOGGING PULLOVER, JACKET

Cut 2

Place on fold

Cut blouse sleeve to here

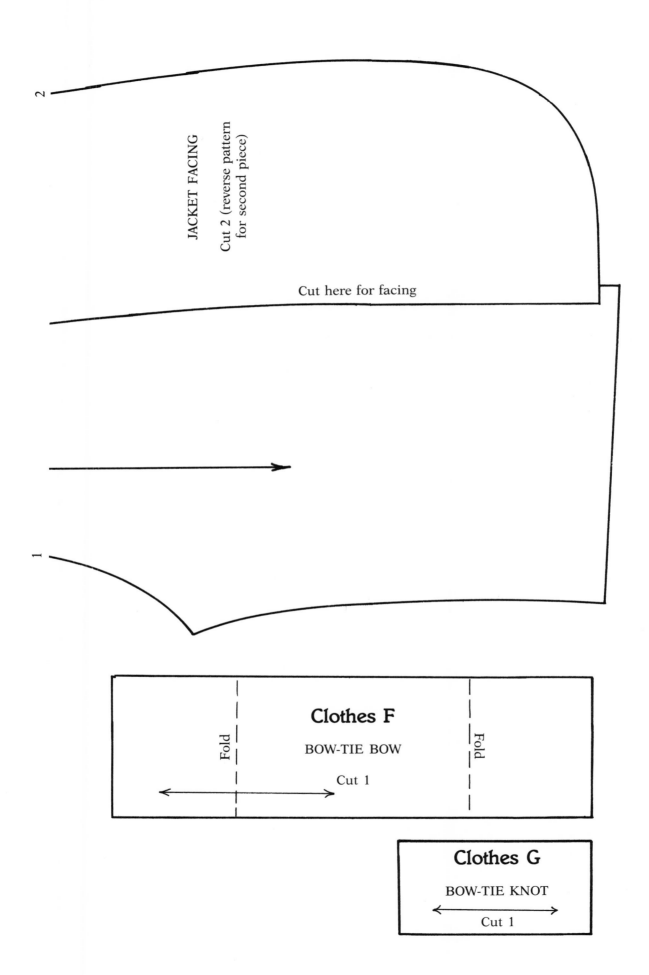

JACKET FACING

Cut 2 (reverse pattern for second piece)

Cut here for facing

2

1

Clothes F

Fold

Fold

BOW-TIE BOW

Cut 1

Clothes G

BOW-TIE KNOT

Cut 1

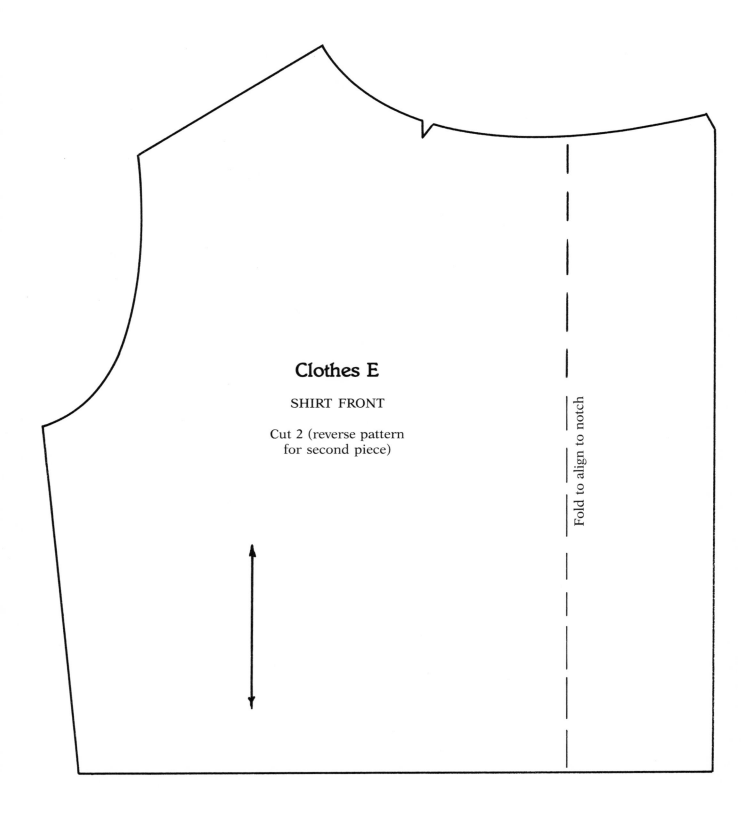

Clothes E

SHIRT FRONT

Cut 2 (reverse pattern
for second piece)

Fold to align to notch

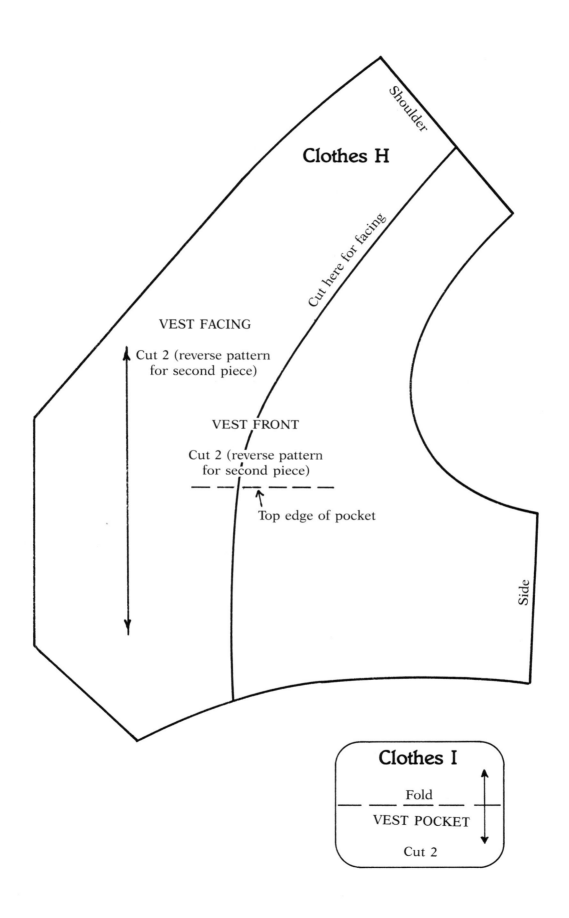

Clothes H

Shoulder

Cut here for facing

VEST FACING

Cut 2 (reverse pattern
for second piece)

VEST FRONT

Cut 2 (reverse pattern
for second piece)

Top edge of pocket

Side

Clothes I

Fold

VEST POCKET

Cut 2

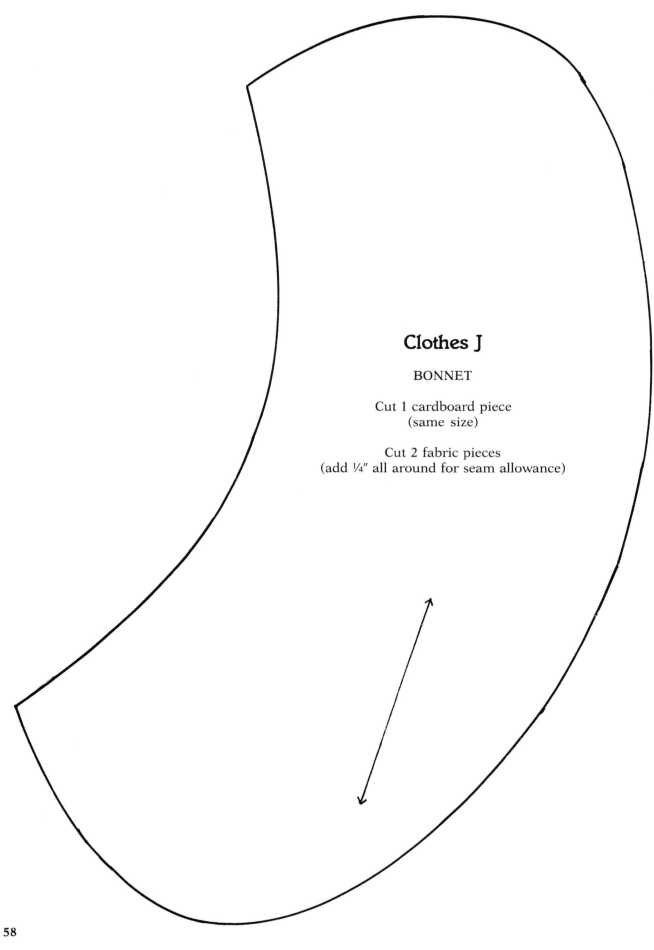

Clothes J

BONNET

Cut 1 cardboard piece
(same size)

Cut 2 fabric pieces
(add ¼″ all around for seam allowance)

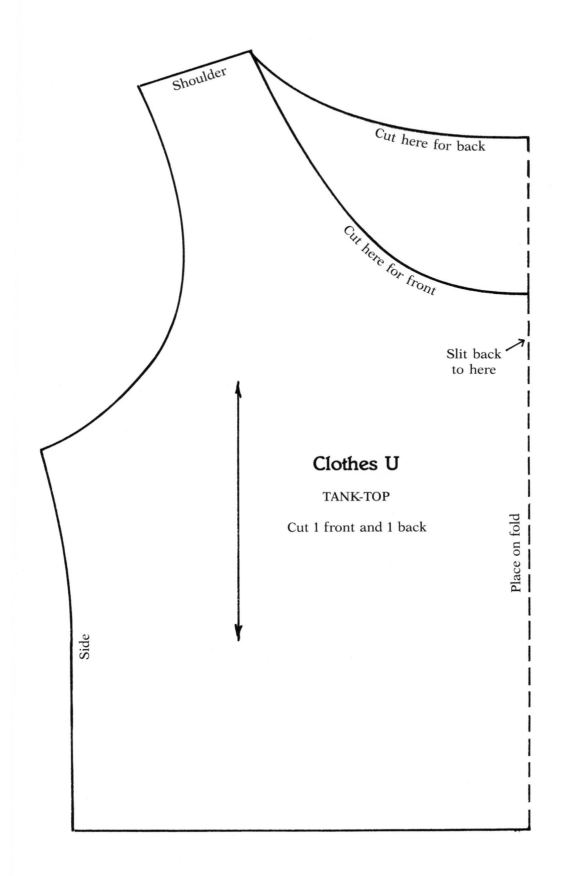

Shoulder

Cut here for back

Cut here for front

Slit back
to here

Clothes U

TANK-TOP

Cut 1 front and 1 back

Place on fold

Side

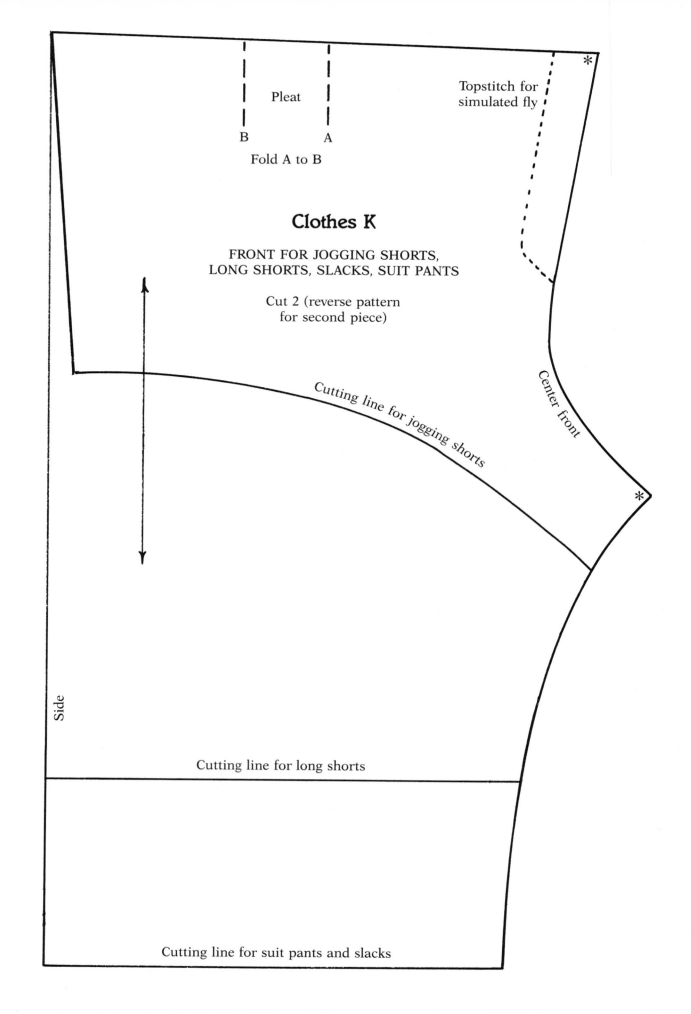

Pleat

B   A

Fold A to B

Topstitch for
simulated fly

Clothes K

**FRONT FOR JOGGING SHORTS,
LONG SHORTS, SLACKS, SUIT PANTS**

Cut 2 (reverse pattern
for second piece)

Cutting line for jogging shorts

Center front

Side

Cutting line for long shorts

Cutting line for suit pants and slacks

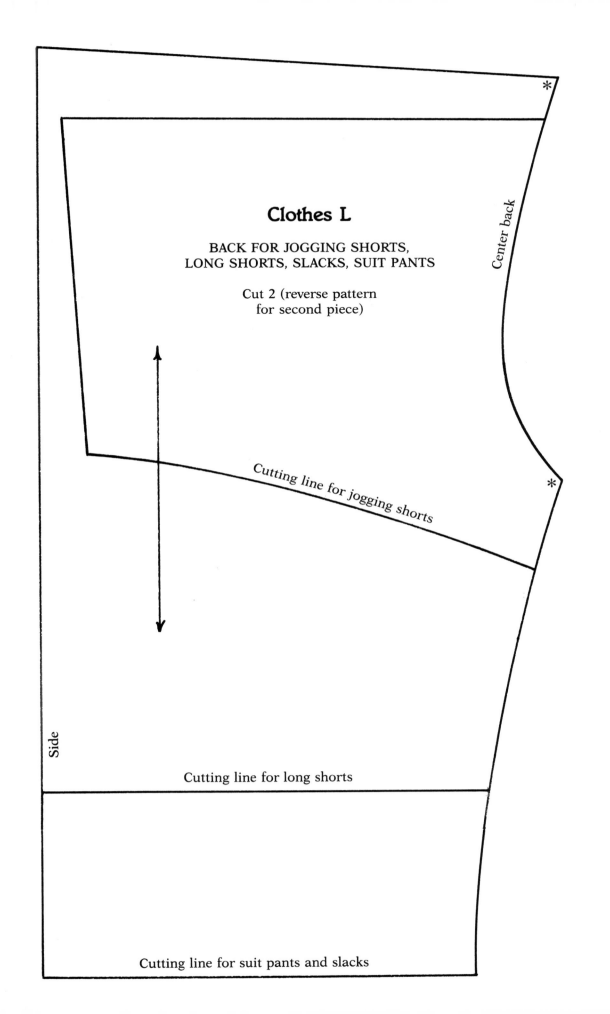

Clothes L

BACK FOR JOGGING SHORTS,
LONG SHORTS, SLACKS, SUIT PANTS

Cut 2 (reverse pattern
for second piece)

Center back

Cutting line for jogging shorts

Side

Cutting line for long shorts

Cutting line for suit pants and slacks

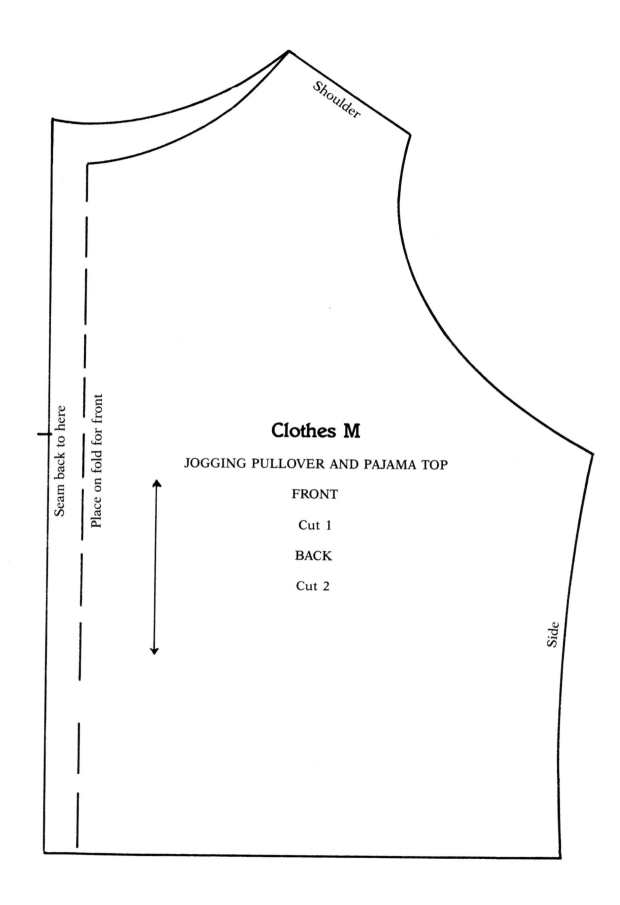

Shoulder

Seam back to here

Place on fold for front

Clothes M

JOGGING PULLOVER AND PAJAMA TOP

FRONT

Cut 1

BACK

Cut 2

Side

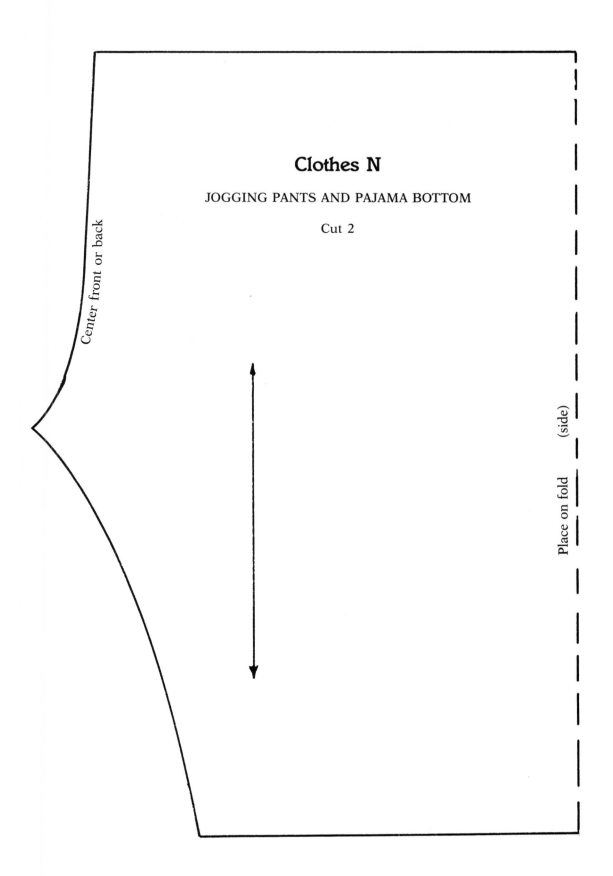

Clothes N

JOGGING PANTS AND PAJAMA BOTTOM

Cut 2

Center front or back

Place on fold (side)

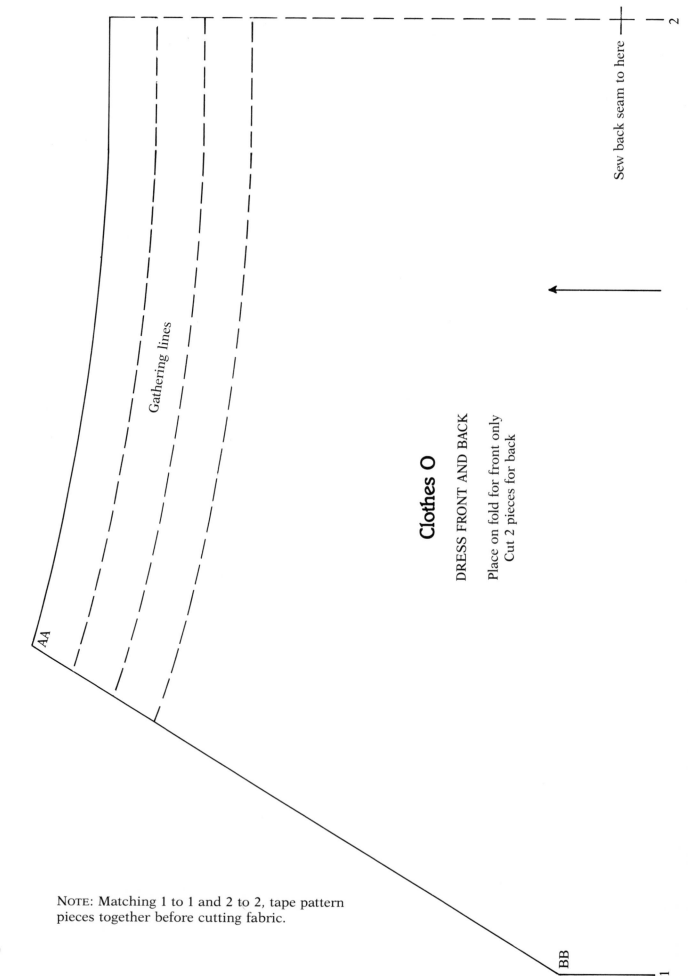

Clothes O

DRESS FRONT AND BACK

Place on fold for front only
Cut 2 pieces for back

Gathering lines

AA

BB

Sew back seam to here

2

1

NOTE: Matching 1 to 1 and 2 to 2, tape pattern
pieces together before cutting fabric.

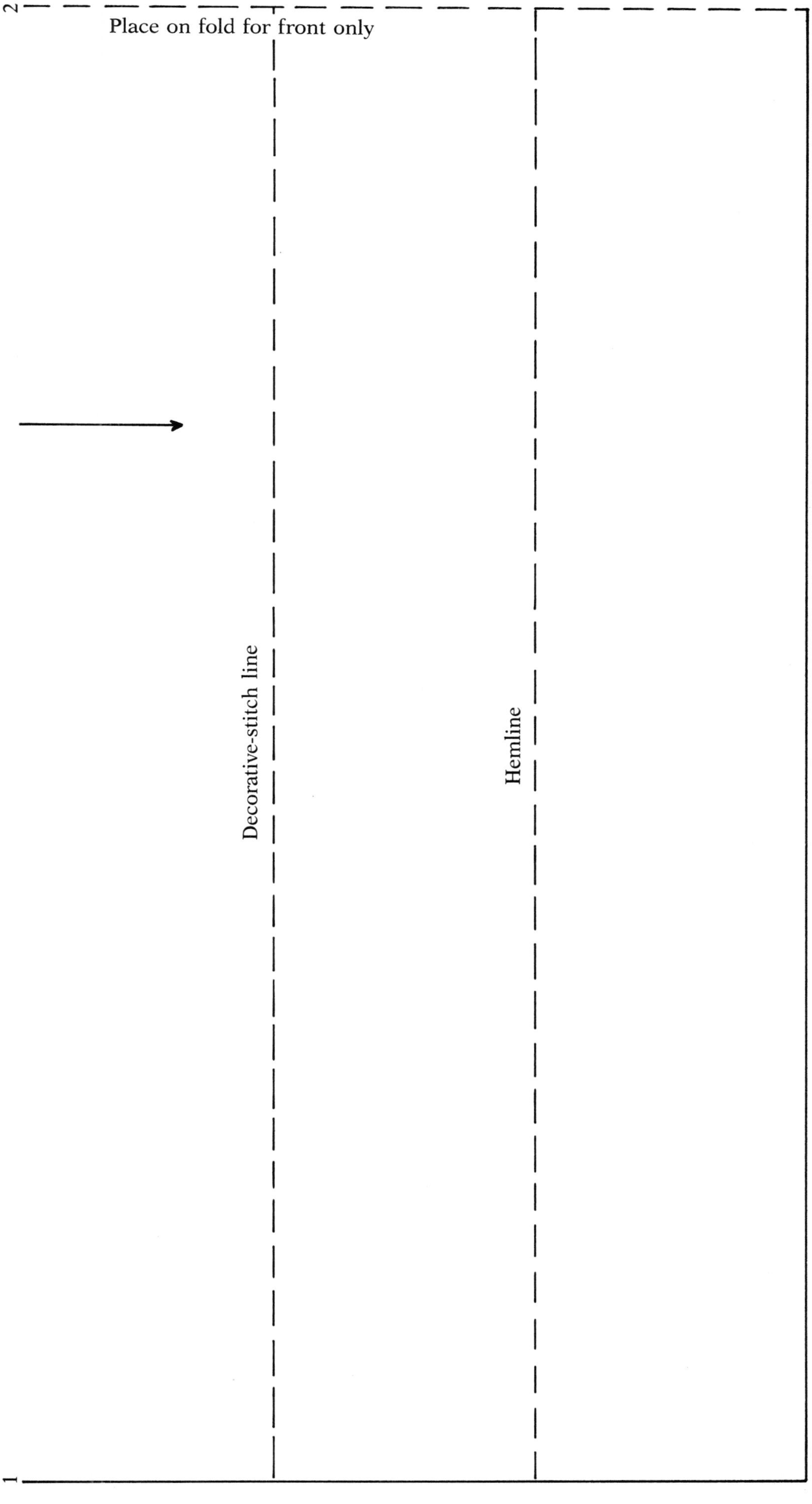

2

Place on fold for front only

→

Decorative-stitch line

Hemline

Place on fold for front only

1

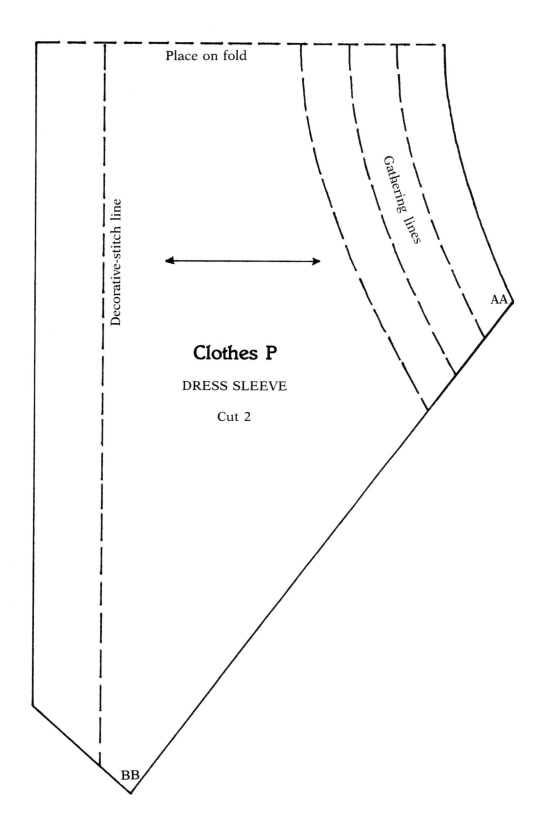

Place on fold

Decorative-stitch line

Gathering lines

AA

Clothes P

DRESS SLEEVE

Cut 2

BB

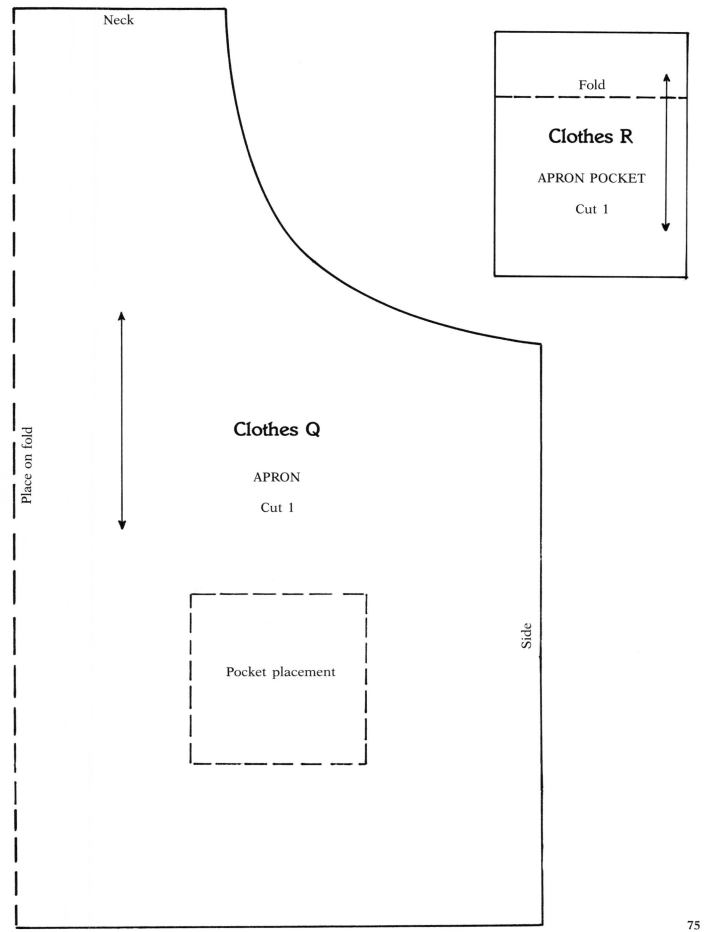

Neck

Place on fold

Clothes Q

APRON

Cut 1

Pocket placement

Side

Fold

Clothes R

APRON POCKET

Cut 1

Note: Matching 1 to 1 and 2 to 2, tape pattern pieces together before cutting fabric.

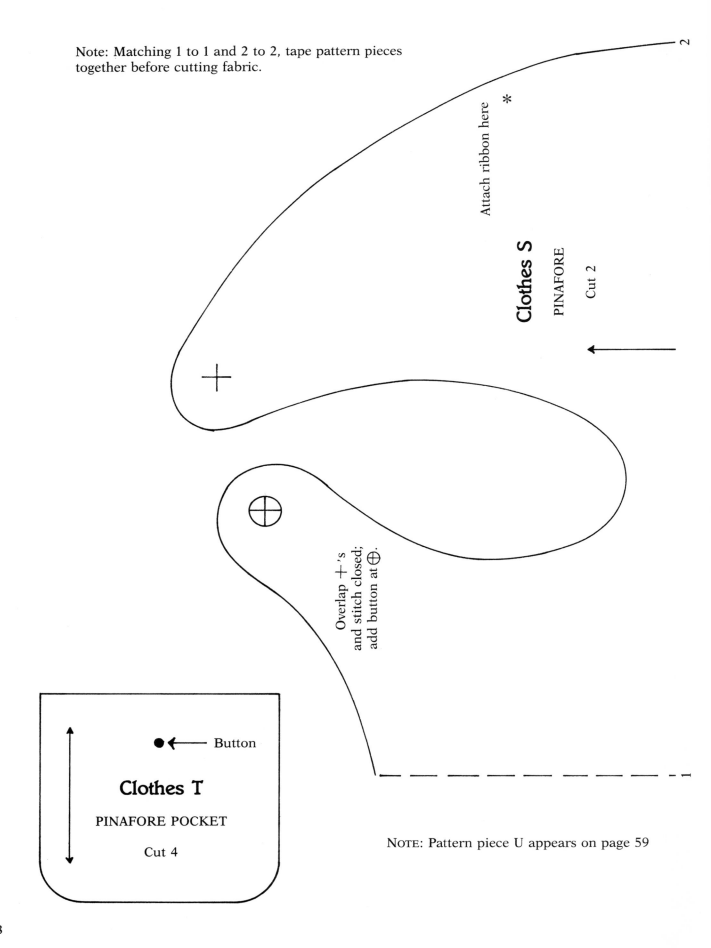

Clothes S

PINAFORE

Cut 2

Attach ribbon here *

Overlap +'s and stitch closed; add button at ⊕.

Clothes T

PINAFORE POCKET

Cut 4

●◄— Button

NOTE: Pattern piece U appears on page 59

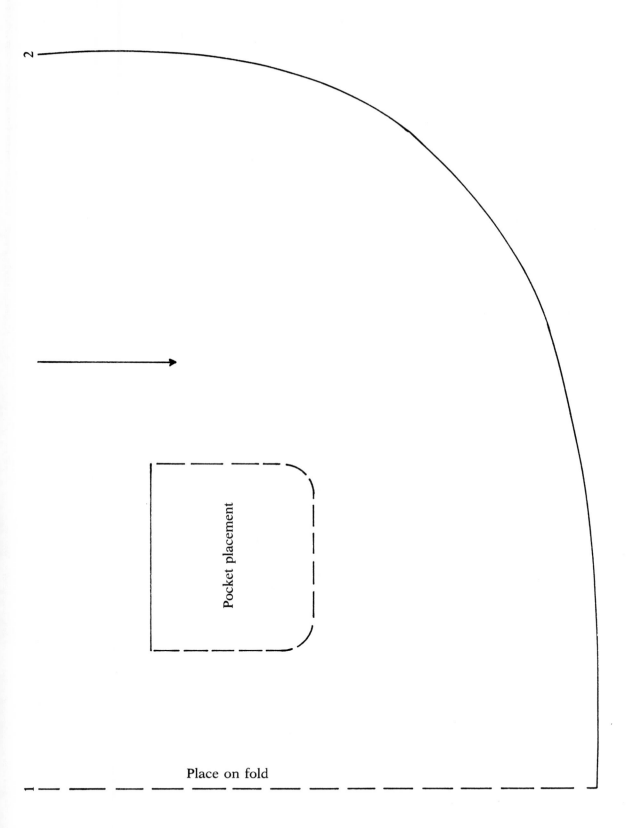

2

Pocket placement

Place on fold

1